overcoming
GIANTS
in your life

Bill Rudge

LIVING TRUTH PUBLISHERS
A Division of Bill Rudge Ministries, Inc.
Hermitage, Pennsylvania

Overcoming the Giants *in Your Life*
Copyright © 2000 by Bill Rudge
ISBN 1-889809-08-X

Published by Living Truth Publishers
A Division of Bill Rudge Ministries, Inc.
Hermitage, Pennsylvania

Cover Design by Jay O. Gould

Printed in the United States of America

Contents

Contents

Introduction

After leaving Egyptian bondage, the goal of the people of Israel was to enter the Promised Land. When they came to the edge of the land the Lord was giving them, Moses sent 12 spies to explore Canaan. These spies came back after 40 days and reported that there were giants in the land.

This account of the 12 spies in the Bible contains crucial insight for us today. Numbers 13 and 14 give an exciting overview of their encounter with giants in the land God promised Israel. That encounter and what followed provide a powerful lesson about God's requirement of faith and obedience by His people—no matter what the circumstance—contrasted with His judgment for their unbelief, murmuring, disobedience, and rebellion.

Just as they were about to reach their goal, Israel encountered giants. Isn't that the way it is? When we're about to achieve our goal and accomplish that which the Lord has led us to do, or when He leads us to step out in faith, we encounter *giants*. If we're not encountering *giants*, then we are, in a sense, back in *Egyptian bondage* and not making our lives really count for the Lord.

The *giants* of today are problems, difficulties, obstacles, opposition, and adverse circumstances that stick their big ugly heads in our faces and try to make us back down in fear and defeat. They want us to murmur, complain, and rebel against the Lord so as to be rendered ineffective.

In contrast, God has a plan and purpose for each of our lives. He has:

- *challenges* He wants us to face
- *valleys* He wants us to go through
- *mountains* He wants us to climb
- *giants* He wants us to defeat
- *obstacles* He wants us to overcome
- *exploits* He wants us to accomplish
- *victories* He wants us to win
- and He wants to do the *impossible* through our lives just as He did in Bible days.

But there are some requirements.

Seek the Lord's Will

The first requirement is that you must seek His will and not your own. People say they want God's will—but do they? Are they willing to invest the time to discover it? Are they willing to pay the price to follow it?

Most of the Israelites only wanted God's will for their lives when it was convenient. When it was inconvenient—like having to fight against giants in order to take the land—they wanted their own will, which, in this situation, was to replace Moses as their leader and go back to Egypt (Numbers 14:1-4).

The people of the community wept and grumbled because they were not willing to obey God's clearly revealed will. In contrast, Moses and Aaron humbly fell face down in front of the whole Israelite assembly (Numbers 14:5) seeking the Lord's guidance and help, and entreating the people not to rebel.

Disobeying the Lord can result in both divine judgment and irreversible lost opportunities. Those murmuring Israelites who were discouraged from entering the Promised Land by the negative report of the 10 faithless spies were not permitted to enter the land. They would wander 40 years in the desert until the whole generation of fighting men 20 years old or more had perished.

God's Blessings Are
Reserved for the Faithful

God's blessings and empowering are reserved for those like Joshua and Caleb, the two faithful spies who wholeheartedly followed the Lord. They received the following reports from the Lord—

> Because my servant Caleb has a different spirit and follows Me wholeheartedly, I will bring him into the land he went to, and his descendants will inherit it (Numbers 14:24).

> Take Joshua son of Nun, a man in whom is the Spirit, and lay your hand on him (Numbers 27:18). He will lead Israel to inherit it (Deuteronomy 1:38).

Years later, the Lord spoke the following words to Joshua shortly before he led the Israelites in the conquest of the Promised Land—

> Be careful to obey all the law my servant Moses gave you; do not turn from it to the right or to the left, that you may be successful wherever you go. Do not let this Book of the Law depart from your mouth; meditate on it day and night, so that you may be careful to do everything written in it. Then you will be prosperous and successful (Joshua 1:7,8).

One of many more Scriptural examples we could cite is David. One of his greatest attributes was his practice of inquiring of the Lord as seen in II Samuel 5:17-19—

> When the Philistines heard that David had been anointed king over Israel, they went up in full force to search for him, but David heard about it and went down to the stronghold.

Now the Philistines had come and spread out in the Valley of Rephaim; so David inquired of the Lord, "Shall I go and attack the Philistines? Will You hand them over to me?" The Lord answered him, "Go, for I will surely hand the Philistines over to you."

As a result of his dependence upon the Lord for help and direction, David won many amazing battles and established a great kingdom.

It is vital that believers today who want to walk in victory must likewise diligently search and obey God's Word. Instead of seeking our own will and trying to manipulate and force God to do what we want, we must seek His will, then obey it. Without this foundational principle, everything we try to accomplish for the Lord will eventually end in futility.

Ask yourself, "Am I willing to fit into God's plan, or do I attempt to make God fit into my plans? Is it truly His will I am seeking to fulfill, or is it really my own?"

When I'm praying for something, I tell people, "If it's not God's will, I don't want it. And if it is His will and I'm being obedient, then nothing can stop me from receiving it. So I have nothing to fear or worry about." I have no will, but to do His will.

Finding God's Direction

While on a Canadian speaking tour in northern Quebec one July, my family and I went on a whale watching trip from a city named Tadoussac. The temperature on land was in the 70's, but over the North Atlantic it was in the 40's and very foggy.

The crew on the boat remained totally silent, cupping their hands over both ears to listen for whales. When someone thought they heard or spotted one, they would yell out the direction. Then the captain would start the engine and go after it. For two hours we chased whales all over the ocean, but most of the time we didn't find any. So we would wait until they supposedly spotted another one, and then go in that direction.

That's the way many Christians seek the Lord's will. They feel like doing such and such, or someone tells them to do this or that, so they run over here. Then when it doesn't work out, God supposedly gives them a new direction, so they attempt something else.

When the crew of that boat really did hear or spot a whale, it was incredible. We were able to get close enough to watch it swim and frolic in the ocean. Likewise, when you hear and obey God's voice, the end result will be most rewarding and victorious.

Instead of chasing the supposed voice of God here and there, we must get on our knees and into His Word so we will know His voice and the direction He has for our lives. Instead of determining what I want God's will to be, then hoping He blesses my decision, I seek the Lord with all my heart through prayer, fasting, and reading Scripture. When I'm certain of what He is leading me to do, I step out in faith and obedience. Until He does give clear direction, I walk by faith using wisdom as I seek to apply Biblical truth and principles. Just as the Israelites stayed right where they were encamped until the Lord led them to move (Numbers 9:18), I, too, usually stay right where I am until the Lord leads otherwise.

Walk by Faith, Not by Sight

When our ministry was still very young, my wife and I were living in an apartment. As the ministry continued to grow, we began looking for a house to move into so we could have our offices in the basement. Instead of opening just one door so we could conveniently walk through it, God opened two doors simultaneously so we would have to make a decision.

One of the houses was very large and ideal for my objectives. The other house was much smaller and not as adequate. Many people said, "Bill, you're a child of the King. You tell God what you want, and He'll give it to you." I replied, "There is something wrong with that. I'm not God. I cannot foresee the future. In my limited foresight, I cannot determine which will ultimately be the best decision. I don't know God's total plan. I walk by faith, not by sight."

Then I said, "What I'm going to do is this: instead of telling God what to do, I'm going to get on my knees. I'm going to pray and fast and find out what His will is, and then I'll be obedient to how He leads. I'll stand and proclaim His will, not my own."

God spoke to my heart to move into the smaller house. In obedience, I did. For months I wondered why. I said, "You know I trust You Lord, but that other house was so much nicer and much more adequate." He spoke to my heart, "Trust Me!"

A few months later, we had 3.7 acres of prime land donated to us. The land, located behind the house we were renting, was appraised at $80,000. Shortly thereafter, the Lord strongly led us to step out in faith and build a ministry center on this property. The Lord intervened in a mighty way, enabling us to overcome many *giants* and complete the building projects without paying any interest. If I had moved into the larger, more adequate house, I would have missed the tremendous blessing and victory God gave to us for obeying His will and not seeking our own.

Do not tell God what you want Him to do. Do not try to force God to do your will. Get on your knees and pray and fast and seek His will. Then stand in faith and persevere until He fulfills what He has led you to do.

Faith – Slayer of Giants

When we decided to build a ministry center on our newly acquired land, a *giant* stepped into our path.

According to the lady who gave out building permits at the city building, we could never build on this property because the land did not fulfill the necessary zoning requirements. She informed us that it was zoned incorrectly for our intentions. She also pointed out that there was no roadway going back to our property which further complicated matters. And finally, she told us that there wasn't enough frontage. Displaying blueprints of our land, she showed us how we could not comply under these conditions. However, she said she would speak to her supervisor.

Naturally, we were somewhat discouraged. Never giving up, however, I fell on my face before the Lord like Moses did and began to pray and fast, knowing that He was able to overcome any obstacle.

The next day when I called her back, she informed me that we would be able to build. They would accept the frontage, but we could only build the ministry center and have outside activities on the commercially zoned land. We would also have to provide our own roadway to our facilities.

Shortly thereafter, a friend of the ministry donated his services to survey the land. He informed us that one-third of our property was already zoned commercially—the exact spot where we wanted to build our ministry center. The other two-thirds, zoned residential, was ideal for building our home. Later we were granted permission to use not only the commercial area, but all of our property for recreational activities.

As he set our boundaries, the surveyor also discovered that a rear delivery entrance to a department store adjacent to our land had been built with a curve and was now partially on our property. This meant that we now owned half of this road, giving us an automatic right to the use of it and meant we didn't have to construct our own road. Indeed the Lord had gone before us and prepared the land.

One Saturday while the volunteers were working on the building, our construction supervisor (who was also donating his services) told me that we needed a crane to lift up the large roof trusses. I had no idea what a roof truss was, let alone where or how to get a crane, so my wife Karen and I sought the Lord. The next week a man stopped at my house after we came home from church. When I opened the door he introduced himself and said, "I'm an ex-alcoholic and God has changed my life. I work for a construction company, and if you ever need a crane, I can get you one for free any Saturday." I told him, "Next Saturday at 9:00 a.m." That Saturday, all the roof trusses for the ministry center were put up.

There have been countless *miracles* in our ministry. Many times people have said, "That is impossible. You cannot achieve this." And they were right—by myself I couldn't. But a sovereign God intervened and altered what appeared to be impossible. He made it possible because we desired His will, not our own. We were walking in obedience to His Word and the leading of His Spirit and seeking to glorify Him.

Another Miracle

On another occasion, we needed a new ministry van. As well as motivating many people to donate finances, the Lord also impressed upon a man's heart in the middle of the night that he should donate an older house and two acres of land he no longer needed so we could sell it and use the money toward a van. The owner of a dealership agreed to sell us the van at cost. Finally, when we were still $2,000 short of the amount we needed, a pastor's wife said the Lord spoke to her heart, and the church her husband pastored filled that gap. It had taken 16 months to raise the funds, but because we sought His will and persevered in faith, the Lord was faithful.

We have witnessed several ministry vehicles being provided throughout the years in similar ways.

Patiently seeking Him for the right vehicle and then trusting Him to provide the funds has been an exciting venture of faith.

Throughout the years we were determined to trust the Lord to meet our needs without borrowing money for which we would have to pay interest. The Lord has always honored us by meeting every need—sometimes on the very last day—even the last hour.

I could share countless illustrations of God's faithfulness and miraculous intervention in my life and ministry. One of many lessons I have learned is:

> Don't try to determine what you want God's will to be. And never attempt to manipulate Him into fulfilling your will. Instead, get on your knees, seek His Word, be sensitive to His Spirit, and then walk in unwavering faith and obedience to His will.

If you do so, you can be assured that it will ultimately end in victory and for His glory.

Keep Your Eyes on the Lord

The Lord had already told Moses He was giving the land of Canaan to the Israelites before the spies explored the land (Numbers 13:1). The fatal flaw of the Israelites was that they allowed their circumstances to remove their focus and trust from the Lord and His promises. They believed the report of the 10 spies rather than the words of God. They compared themselves to the giants instead of trusting Almighty God. Thus, their unbelief resulted in fear, complaining, and rebellion. In contrast, Joshua and Caleb, two of the 12 spies, kept their focus on the Lord. They tore their clothes and said to the entire Israelite assembly—

The land we passed through and explored is exceedingly good. If the Lord is pleased with us, He will lead us into that land, a land flowing with milk and honey, and will give it to us. Only do not rebel against the Lord. And do not be afraid of the people of the land, because we will swallow them up. Their protection is gone, but the Lord is with us. Do not be afraid of them (Numbers 14:7-9).

Keeping your eyes on your problems and circumstances is like holding a small penny so close to your eye that it blots out everything else—flowers, trees, sun, and horizon. When I focus on my circumstances, I get discouraged. It is easy to complain and murmur because sometimes there is so much opposition and so many obstacles. But when you hold that penny back from your eye and get it in proper perspective, you realize that it is extremely small in comparison to your surroundings. So too, when we keep our eyes on our problems, they loom very large in our sight, but when we keep our eyes on the Lord and His promises, we realize His power and faithfulness will enable us to overcome any *giant.* What we fear is often not as ferocious as what we anticipate.

My wife and I were staying at an Army officer's house at the Presidio of Monterey in California where I had been ministering for various chapel services. During our free time we enjoyed walking down the hill through the base to Monterey Bay. The officer and his wife who sponsored me and with whom we were staying had told us that a mountain lion had recently been sighted on the property and warned us to be careful after dusk. They offered us the use of their vehicle, but preferring to walk, we declined their gracious offer.

One evening about dusk, Karen and I were walking back up the long steep hill to the captain's house. We came to a clearing by a wooded area when Karen screamed in terror, "Mountain lion!" She saw two eyes glaring at us in the dark. Quickly I turned to evaluate the situation, but laughed as I informed her it was only a house cat.

Upon our return a year later to speak again at the Presidio, the captain, his wife, Karen, and I laughed whenever we saw a cat, remembering how startled and momentarily paralyzed with fear Karen had become.

There are *giants* we face that are more figments of our imagination than the real thing, but they are just as paralyzing. When Karen saw glowing eyes in the dark, there was no question in her mind at the time that we had come face to face with a ferocious mountain lion.

Unlike the mountain lion episode, however, many of the *giants* we face are real. David fought against the real giant, Goliath, but kept his trust in the Lord. His faith in God was memorialized in I Samuel 17:45-47 as he spoke to Goliath—

> You come against me with sword and spear and javelin, but I come against you in the name of the Lord Almighty, the God of the armies of Israel, whom you have defied.
>
> This day the Lord will hand you over to me, and I'll strike you down and cut off your head. Today I will give the carcasses of the Philistine army to the birds of the air and the beasts of the earth, and the whole world will know that there is a God in Israel.
>
> All those gathered here will know that it is not by sword or spear that the Lord saves; for the battle is the Lord's, and He will give all of you into our hands.

Oftentimes, I am in circumstances in which there are no apparent solutions. All options seem impossible—or at least undesirable. At these times, I have learned to fall on my face and cry out to the Lord. I look to the only One who can resolve the seemingly impossible situations.

Psalm 121:1,2 encourages us—

> I lift up my eyes to the hills—where does my help come from? My help comes from the Lord, the Maker of heaven and earth.

After determining what I believe to be the definite direction of the Lord, I trust Him to fulfill what He has led me to do. I strive to keep my eyes on Him, not my circumstances. Then when I'm in the midst of adversity, I have the assurance that I am in His will and that He will ultimately work the situation out to accomplish His purpose.

When Circumstances Seem Contrary

The spies came back from the land of Canaan and reported to Moses and the whole Israelite community that the land did flow with milk and honey (Numbers 13:27). However, they didn't anticipate the people living there would be so powerful and the cities so large and fortified (Numbers 13:28). The circumstances were contrary to what they had expected or hoped.

A few years after we completed our first building project, a friend of the ministry told me that he wanted to donate his services to build a large addition to the ministry center. I began to seek the Lord through prayer and fasting to be sure He was leading us to do so and to have the assurance He would meet the needs.

Two months later, I was certain that the Lord wanted us to step out in faith and begin. But as soon as we did, everything went wrong. It looked like we wouldn't get the necessary land rezoned so we could build our addition. We were also facing many other difficulties. To make matters worse, our funds got so tight, it did not even appear we could cover the ministry expenses, let alone complete an extensive building project.

A little more than a year after stepping out in total faith and facing many overwhelming obstacles, and with virtually all volunteer labor, the Lord once again made the impossible a reality. Because we sought and obeyed His will, He enabled us to build a ministry complex—valued at over half-a-million dollars—without a penny of interest being paid.

What I Learned from Moses

During this time of being assaulted by *giants*, I said, "Lord, I am being obedient to what You have led me to do. What's happening?" As I sought the Lord, He impressed upon my heart the account of Moses leading the Israelites out of Egyptian bondage. Where did God lead them? Right to the Red Sea.

They were hemmed in by the uncrossable Red Sea and mountains, with Pharaoh's hordes coming from behind to annihilate them. Don't you feel like that sometimes? There have been numerous times when I thought God had forsaken me, and I felt hopeless. I wondered, "What good can come out of this?" I wanted to murmur and complain. I wanted to escape. But you cannot see the impossible unless you are in an impossible situation. Be faithful to God, and if in doing so you end up hemmed in by the enemy, be at peace and know that He is God. Trust Him to deliver you.

Moses didn't get to the Red Sea by mistake. God purposely led Moses and Israel to that impossible situation and boxed them in so that He could be glorified through what He was about to do.

God spoke to my heart through the account of Moses. He allowed us to also be boxed in on all sides with nowhere to turn, making an addition totally impossible, so that when it was completed, He would be the One who was glorified.

The local commissioners voted unanimously to rezone the land. The Lord raised up over 200 groups, churches, businesses, and individuals who donated funds, materials, and labor. The head of the construction project was the very same man who, while we were working on our first building, came by and said, "Something keeps telling me to come back and help." He assisted on the first building, and then God gave him the vision to build the large addition.

There are many exciting illustrations, too numerous to mention here, concerning how God provided the ministry complex. In the midst of God's great blessing and apparent interventions there were also tremendous obstacles—and one *giant* after another.

When we built the first ministry center, after the foundation footers were dug, we had to wait three weeks to pour the cement. The footers filled with rain water and none of the three pumps would work. A wall caved in twice—and sat for a couple of months. The easement pipe was rejected three times. We were continually out of funds. We waited many months for a bricklayer. Our parking lot had to be dug up in the middle of winter due to an underground waterline leak. The problems continued.

The murmurers and complainers arose, saying, "Are you sure the Lord told you to do this? You'll never do it." But we did. God fulfilled what He had led us to do. We dared to trust Him to overcome what seemed to be insurmountable obstacles, and He was faithful.

When the time came to relocate—after facing almost as many *giants* leaving the land as entering it—the ministry center would become a double blessing. First, it blessed us for 18 years by providing the means for fulfilling the vision the Lord had given us up until that point. The sale of it would bless the ministry again by providing greatly needed funds for the continued expansion of our growing international outreach. It would enable us to take advantage of opportunities that over 22 years of faithful ministry have opened to us—providing the potential to impact literally millions of lives for Christ.

The pattern I see in Scripture is what I have witnessed in my life and ministry over and over again. The Lord leads me to do something, or I spend time seeking Him until His leading is clear. Then I step out in faith and obedience, and most of the time just about everything imaginable goes wrong. It seems impossible to be fulfilled, and defeat seems apparent. Then the Lord intervenes in His time and way, and is faithful to bring ultimate victory. He has done this countless times.

God's Mighty Interventions

An upcoming book entitled, *The Impossible*, documents some of the miraculous interventions the Lord has done in my life and ministry. The amazing accounts listed below will be included.

- With no money, staff, or facilities, my wife Karen and I started what was to become a growing international outreach ministry.
- By stepping out in total faith and obedience, a ministry center valued at over half-a-million dollars was built without a penny of interest being paid.
- During the 10 years we sponsored special outdoor outreaches, God kept them from ever being rained out, sometimes through amazing weather occurrences.
- The Lord has fulfilled 100% of what I have publicly proclaimed that He has led me to do, much of which seemed totally impossible to fulfill.

God's intervention in apparently impossible circumstances resulted in dozens of documented *miracles*. I have been:

- threatened and attacked
- "prophesied" against for my destruction and had spells put on me
- put on "hit lists"

- in frequent situations of extreme danger and surrounded in ghettos and foreign countries
- nearly frozen to death in New Mexico
- almost blinded when a car battery exploded in my face
- nearly shot at a cult complex in West Virginia
- "terrorized" in an Arab country
- almost killed three times in Colorado
- in a plane circling above Syracuse airport in the midst of one of the worst electrical storms known to that area
- hopelessly stranded in India
- almost killed by a bus in the Himalayas
- in Haiti during a coup attempt
- able to lead a feared voodoo witch doctor to the Lord, during which time I was protected from being killed by three angry men armed with machetes and a lead pipe
- the target of a failed robbery attempt in Lagos, Nigeria
- smuggled in and out of a country where it is forbidden to share the Gospel under penalty of possible prison or death sentence
- nearly stranded in Africa
- in several near-tragic accidents, including a violent four-vehicle collision while traveling through Oregon after ministering in British Columbia
- faced with numerous other potentially danger- ous and deadly circumstances, but the God of the Bible has always intervened, delivered, and brought the ultimate victory.

Truly, God's dealings in my life and ministry pre- sent a tremendous witness of His mercy, faithfulness, protection, and power.

Some of you might say, "Bill, what are you doing wrong that all these things are happening?" It's not what I'm doing wrong, it's what we're doing right.

"Hard Pressed on Every Side, but Not Crushed"

The apostle Paul was beaten, stoned, imprisoned, and shipwrecked. He experienced hunger, thirst, and cold, and was often in danger of death (II Corinthians 11:23-33), but the end result was always victory, and his life was not taken until God's purpose was fulfilled.

II Corinthians 6:4-10—

...in great endurance; in troubles, hardships and distresses; in beatings, imprisonments and riots; in hard work, sleepless nights and hunger...through glory and dishonor, bad report and good report; genuine, yet regarded as impostors; known, yet regarded as unknown; dying, and yet we live on; beaten, and yet not killed; sorrowful, yet always rejoicing; poor, yet making many rich; having nothing, and yet possessing everything.

II Corinthians 4:8-10—

We are hard pressed on every side, but not crushed; perplexed, but not in despair; persecuted, but not abandoned; struck down, but not destroyed. We always carry around in our body the death of Jesus, so that the life of Jesus may also be revealed in our body.

Psalm 44 is intriguing. It begins with the psalmist recounting God's faithfulness and the victories He provided. Then at verse 9 it completely changes. The psalmist is bewildered, because even though the people of God have not forsaken the Lord, it appears as though God has abandoned them.

Let's read this relevant psalm and then see what insight we might gain from the apostle Paul's quote from it in Romans 8:36.

Psalm 44:1-26—

We have heard with our ears, O God; our fathers have told us what You did in their days, in days long ago. With Your hand You drove out the nations and planted our fathers; You crushed the peoples and made our fathers flourish. It was not by their sword that they won the land, nor did their arm bring them victory; it was Your right hand, Your arm, and the light of Your face, for You loved them. You are my King and my God, who decrees victories for Jacob. Through You we push back our enemies; through Your name we trample our foes. I do not trust in my bow, my sword does not bring me victory; but You give us victory over our enemies, You put our adversaries to shame. In God we make our boast all day long, and we will praise Your name forever. Selah

But now You have rejected and humbled us; You no longer go out with our armies. You made us retreat before the enemy, and our adversaries have plundered us. You gave us up to be devoured like sheep and have scattered us among the nations. You sold Your people for a pittance, gaining nothing from their sale. You have made us a reproach to our neighbors, the scorn and derision of those around us. You have made us a byword among the nations; the peoples shake their heads at us. My disgrace is before me all day long, and my face is covered with shame at the taunts of those who reproach and revile me, because of the enemy, who is bent on revenge.

All this happened to us, though we had not forgotten You or been false to Your covenant. Our hearts had not turned back; our feet had not strayed from Your path. But You crushed us and made us a haunt for jackals and covered us over with deep darkness.

If we had forgotten the name of our God or spread out our hands to a foreign god, would not God have discovered it, since He knows the secrets of the heart? Yet for Your sake we face death all day long; we are considered as sheep to be slaughtered.

Awake, O Lord! Why do You sleep? Rouse Yourself! Do not reject us forever. Why do You hide Your face and forget our misery and oppression? We are brought down to the dust; our bodies cling to the ground. Rise up and help us; redeem us because of Your unfailing love.

God's Ways Are Not Our Ways

Has God forgotten us? Of course not. He has a broader perspective and purpose than our immediate circumstance and limited view.

The apostle Paul, contemplating the suffering and adversity of the early Church, asks some relevant questions in Romans 8:31,35—

...If God is for us, who can be against us? Who shall separate us from the love of Christ? Shall trouble or hardship or persecution or famine or nakedness or danger or sword?

In the context of the suffering believer, Paul continues in Romans 8:36 by quoting from Psalm 44:22—

As it is written: "For Your sake we face death all day long; we are considered as sheep to be slaughtered."

Yet, Paul goes on to say in Romans 8:37-39—

No, in all these things we are more than conquerors through Him who loved us. For I am convinced that neither death nor life, neither angels nor demons, neither the present nor the future, nor any powers, neither height nor depth, nor anything else in all creation, will be able to separate us from the love of God that is in Christ Jesus our Lord.

Whether we are being blessed or whether we are suffering and facing adversity, our faith in Christ enables us to be more than conquerors. In spite of frustration and seeming defeat, we can be assured that God is faithfully working behind the scenes to fulfill His purpose.

After having our car totaled in a four-vehicle collision in Oregon, the Lord gave me Psalm 34:19—

Many are the afflictions of the righteous; but the Lord delivers him out of them all (NAS).

As David in his old age made an oath concerning Solomon becoming king, he testified of God's faithfulness when he stated in I Kings 1:29 how the Lord had delivered him out of every trouble.

II Timothy 3:10-12—

You, however, know all about my teaching, my way of life, my purpose, faith, patience, love, endurance, persecutions, sufferings—what kinds of things happened to me in Antioch, Iconium and Lystra, the persecutions I endured. Yet the Lord rescued me from all of them. In fact, everyone who wants to live a godly life in Christ Jesus will be persecuted.

Some people say to me, "Aren't you afraid when you travel, with the car wrecks, train derailments, plane crashes, bombs, terrorists, hijackings, riots, threats of war, disease, and the other potential dangers you have faced?" I answer, "No. The reason I go and risk my life is because I believe the safest place to be is in God's will." Before I go on any missionary outreach, I pray and fast for the Lord's direction. No matter what happens, I have the assurance that God has it all in control.

As Psalm 138:7 states:

> Though I walk in the midst of trouble, You preserve my life; You stretch out Your hand against the anger of my foes, with Your right hand You save me.

Yes, I often face hardships, difficulties, and impossible situations, but the Lord has delivered me from them all and has eventually brought ultimate victory. The Lord has given me the assurance that my life will not be taken until His purpose is fulfilled. If His purpose for my life is fulfilled before He returns, then I can also trust Him to give me the grace to face death.

Look to God, Not the Circumstances

If Noah had gone by circumstances, he would have never built the ark. If Moses had gone by circumstances, he would have never crossed the Red Sea. If David had gone by circumstances, he would have never faced Goliath. If Elijah had gone by circumstances, he would not have taken on the prophets of Baal. If Daniel had gone by circumstances, he would have denied the Lord, and thereby escaped the lions' den.

Throughout God's Word many believers refused to allow adverse circumstances and the enemy to back them down in fear and defeat. They stood in faith and trust and were enabled by God to be victorious— some by doing great exploits; others, by being faithful even unto death (Hebrews 11).

In molding and bringing His children to maturity and faith, God uses different circumstances for different people. For example, to temper and develop Joseph's character, God used the experience of being cast into a pit by his jealous brothers and being sold into slavery and imprisonment. With Moses, God used 40 years in Egypt and 40 years in the wilderness to develop his skills of leadership.

Evaluation Time

I tell someone going through a difficult time of discouragement and defeat that the first thing I do is to evaluate my walk with the Lord. Realizing that God honors those who honor Him, I would make certain there is no aspect of sin or disobedience which is resulting in the Lord allowing this apparent defeat.

That not being the case, I would then seek the Lord as to whether what I am involved with is according to His will for my life. Often, the commitment of time and energy may be to good causes, but it is not the purpose and priority He has for one's life. As a result, frustration is experienced.

It could be that God is using these circumstances to develop your character and mold and make you into what He wants.

I Peter 4:12-19—

> Dear friends, do not be surprised at the painful trial you are suffering, as though something strange were happening to you. But rejoice that you participate in the sufferings of Christ, so that you may be overjoyed when His glory is revealed. If you are insulted because of the name of Christ, you are blessed, for the Spirit of glory and of God rests on you....So then, those who suffer according to God's will should commit themselves to their faithful Creator and continue to do good.

Persevere in Faith and Be Used by God

God's work is accomplished, not by those who give up when the obstacles and difficulties arise, but by those who endure the *pit* and *wilderness* experiences set before them.

There is often one major difference between the person God uses and the one God doesn't use. While both may greatly desire to be used, the one who gives up easily when obstacles and difficulties arise never seems to be effectively used by God. In contrast, the one who endures and goes *through the fire* is the one God eventually greatly uses for His glory.

Let me explain it another way. It's sort of like the Lord saying, "I want you to follow Me." You look ahead and see a beautiful meadow. So you say, "Oh, Lord, I'll follow You anywhere!" But as you follow the Lord, you eventually come to a deep, dark valley, a barren wilderness, or a high, steep mountain. You may stop and exclaim, "Wait a minute, Lord. It's too hard. I didn't expect this. This is as far as I go!"

If only you would have continued through that deep, dark valley or barren wilderness, or up that steep mountain, you could have viewed the other side. There, you would have come to lush, green grass, cool and crystal-clear water, and the fulfillment of God's promise and blessing.

Many believers never get past the obstacles and difficulties. They will never hear, "Well done, thou good and faithful servant," or experience the joy and excitement of those who persevere and remain faithful to the end.

Watch the Gauges...
Your Life Depends on It!

Several years ago, I received a special gift from my wife—an hour-long airplane flight in which I would pilot the plane. This was thrilling because I had never flown an airplane before. I climbed into a little Tomahawk plane and the instructor explained what to do. He then informed me that it was time for me to fly it without his help.

I pulled the throttle down. We started down the runway and picked up speed. I pulled the steering wheel back and we began to lift off the runway. Once we were in the air he said, "You turn the steering wheel to the right to go right, and to the left to go left. Pull it back if you want to go up, and push it in if you want to go down."

That sounded easy enough, but it wasn't. I had to use my left hand to steer—because my right hand had to stay on the throttle. Being right-handed, I pulled the steering wheel back too hard with my left hand, and we started flying straight up in the air. So I pushed it in, but again too hard, and we started to nosedive. I would turn too far left or right and we would go sideways. I was sweating and my heart was pounding, but the instructor would not help me.

Finally, after getting used to the controls, I started looking out the window to enjoy the scenery and to determine where I was going. I was totally disoriented. Before I knew it, I was flying sideways again and going in the wrong direction.

The instructor taught me two important flying principles to enable me to keep going in the right direction and to keep us headed toward the ministry center to take aerial pictures. He said, "First, keep your eyes focused on the horizon. Second, watch your gauges and trust them no matter what you think or feel."

The Lord taught me that keeping my eyes focused on the horizon is similar to keeping my eyes focused on Him. Watching and trusting the gauges is comparable to reading and obeying God's Word. When we do, we'll always go in the right direction.

God's Time and Way

The Israelites had a much different scenario in mind concerning when and how the conquest of the Promised Land would occur than what actually transpired. They initially backed down from entering the land when they were supposed to because they were afraid of the giants who were living there. Then because of their unbelief and rebellion, God pronounced that all of them 20 years old or more who grumbled against Him would wander 40 years in the desert until they perished.

Numbers 14:39-45 tells what happened next—

When Moses reported this to all the Israelites, they mourned bitterly. Early the next morning they went up toward the high hill country. "We have sinned," they said. "We will go up to the place the Lord promised."

But Moses said, "Why are you disobeying the Lord's command? This will not succeed! Do not go up, because the Lord is not with you. You will be defeated by your enemies, for the Amalekites and Canaanites will face you there. Because you have turned away from the Lord, He will not be with you and you will fall by the sword."

Nevertheless, in their presumption they went up toward the high hill country, though neither Moses nor the ark of the Lord's covenant moved from the camp. Then the Amalekites and Canaanites who lived in that hill country came down and attacked them and beat them down all the way to Hormah.

At first the Israelites didn't want to do it God's way. Then they didn't want to do it in God's time. They discovered that to have His empowerment and blessing, the Lord requires His children to do it both in His time and way.

No Shortcut to Spiritual Maturity

People are impatient by nature and don't like to face adversity. We want what we want when we want it, which is usually *now!* We just don't like to wait and we don't like to be inconvenienced. So too, we want God to instantly answer our prayers and immediately solve all of our problems. When He doesn't, we think He has failed us. Many become discouraged because they have tried every available formula and technique but haven't achieved the promised results. That's because there is no shortcut to spiritual maturity. To grow in Christ and be conformed to His likeness takes time.

God can and does work instantly and supernaturally, but He usually works in time. The following are examples of God's dealings with His people over time.

Noah was told to build an ark because there was going to be a flood. If Noah had looked only at his circumstances instead of trusting in the words of God, he would have given up in defeat. What he did took considerable faith. He built a large boat on dry land.

He foretold a phenomenon—rain—that had never occurred before. "But there went up a mist from the earth, and watered the whole face of the ground" (Genesis 2:6—KJV). He preached for 120 years and failed to win one convert. Yet, in God's time and way it was fulfilled.

> By faith Noah, when warned about things not yet seen, in holy fear built an ark to save his family (Hebrews 11:7).

The people of Noah's day may have laughed and sneered, but as Jesus said, "The flood came and destroyed them all" (Luke 17:27). And as II Peter 2:5 states—

> ...He [God] did not spare the ancient world when He brought the flood on its ungodly people, but protected Noah, a preacher of righteousness, and seven others.

God promised Abraham a son, but after many years of delay it appeared hopeless. Yet, Romans 4:18-21 victoriously states—

> Against all hope, Abraham in hope believed and so became the father of many nations, just as it had been said to him, "So shall your offspring be." Without weakening in his faith, he faced the fact that his body was as good as dead—since he was about a hundred years old—and that Sarah's womb was also dead. Yet he did not waver through unbelief regarding the promise of God, but was strengthened in his faith and gave glory to God, being fully persuaded that God had power to do what he had promised.

At the age of 17 (Genesis 37:2), Joseph had a dream that his brothers would bow down to him. His brothers threw him into a pit and sold him as a slave into Egypt. Then in Egypt, he was put in prison for honoring the Lord and spurning the affection of Potiphar's wife. Sometimes we are persecuted and face problems, not for doing what is wrong, but for doing what is right and seeking to live totally for the Lord. God never said it would be easy.

God allowed 13 years to pass while He prepared Joseph. Eventually—in God's time and way—the dream He gave Joseph was fulfilled. Joseph became second-in-command under Pharaoh in Egypt at age 30 (Genesis 41:46). At age 37 (20 years after his dream and being sold as a slave), his brothers bowed before him, fulfilling the dream and saving Israel from starvation. Two years later, he revealed his identity to his brothers—and later to his father Jacob who had been led to believe that Joseph died years earlier.

Psalm 105:17-19 says it this way—

And He sent a man before them—Joseph, sold as a slave. They bruised his feet with shackles, his neck was put in irons, till what he foretold came to pass, till the word of the Lord proved him true.

For 80 years, God prepared Moses to deliver the Hebrews out of Egyptian bondage and give them His Law. Then the following 40 years were filled with difficulties as Moses led the wandering Israelites in the wilderness between Sinai and Canaan. However, God used Moses to mold a complaining, unbelieving, and rebellious people into the nation of Israel. Moses died at age 120 after leading God's people from the slave labor camps of Egypt to the edge of the Promised Land. There are references to Moses in nearly every book in the Bible.

Naomi's husband and two sons died in Moab. Her two daughters-in-law were left childless. Upon returning to her hometown of Bethlehem, she told the women there—

Don't call me Naomi, call me Mara, because the Almighty has made my life very bitter. I went away full, but the Lord has brought me back empty. Why call me Naomi? The Lord has afflicted me; the Almighty has brought misfortune upon me (Ruth 1:20,21).

Little did Naomi know that she would experience triumph through tragedy. The Lord had a purpose and would eventually use Ruth, her Moabitess daughter-in-law, to marry Boaz and become an ancestor of the Messiah.

Ruth 4:13-17 gives the following account—

So Boaz took Ruth and she became his wife. Then he went to her, and the Lord enabled her to conceive, and she gave birth to a son. The women said to Naomi: "Praise be to the Lord, who this day has not left you without a kinsman-redeemer. May he become famous throughout Israel! He will renew your life and sustain you in your old age. For your daughter-in-law, who loves you and who is better to you than seven sons, has given him birth." Then Naomi took the child, laid him in her lap and cared for him. The women living there said, "Naomi has a son." And they named him Obed. He was the father of Jesse, the father of David (Ruth 4:13-17).

Year after year, Hannah was provoked by her rival Peninnah, because the Lord had closed Hannah's womb. In bitterness of soul, Hannah prayed to the Lord in the tabernacle for a son. Eli the priest observed her praying silently and misunderstood, thinking she had been drinking wine. Upon Hannah's explanation of praying out of great anguish and grief, Eli answered, "May the God of Israel grant you what you have asked of Him" (I Samuel 1:17). In the course of time, Hannah gave birth to a son, Samuel. After weaning Samuel, she brought him to the house of the Lord at Shiloh and said to Eli—

> As surely as you live, my lord, I am the woman who stood here beside you praying to the Lord. I prayed for this child, and the Lord has granted me what I asked of Him. So now I give him to the Lord. For his whole life he will be given over to the Lord (1 Samuel 1:26-28).

God used David's years as a shepherd, during which he had encounters with a lion and a bear, to prepare him for facing the giant Goliath. From his youth, David was prepared to be king of Israel and was a man after God's own heart. David was anointed by Samuel to replace Saul as king. But what happened? For years, Saul pursued David, trying to kill him. He had to flee and hide in caves just to save his life. Eventually, David became the greatest king in Israel's history.

Jeremiah the prophet faithfully prophesied for 40 years during the final days of Judah's apostasy (prior to their Babylonian captivity). He was lonely, misunderstood, accused of treason, beaten, frequently imprisoned, and cast into a muddy cistern and left to starve to death, but he was rescued and his prophecies were ultimately fulfilled.

The angel Gabriel told Mary her Son Jesus would be great and receive the throne of David and would reign over the house of Jacob forever (Luke 1:26-35). Yet, she saw Him die on a cross. I am sure she expected a much different scenario than transpired, but according to Scripture, all will be fulfilled at His Second Coming.

Jesus taught the disciples for three years before they were prepared to carry out His great commission. They were perplexed and fearful when He was crucified, but became bold witnesses when empowered by the Holy Spirit after His resurrection.

The apostle John faithfully served Christ into his old age. He was exiled on the island of Patmos because of the Word of God and his testimony for Jesus. While there the Lord gave him the visions and prophecies of the book of Revelation.

Why Does It Take So Long?

I don't know why God sometimes takes so long before He fulfills His promises or answers the cry of the righteous. I don't know why it took 120 years before God fulfilled His word to Noah that He would destroy the world by a flood. I don't know why God allowed Abraham and Sarah to wait 25 years before He fulfilled His promise of Isaac (Genesis 12:2-4; 21:5). I don't know why God allowed Joseph to go through 13 years of difficulties before He fulfilled the dream He had given him. I don't know why Moses had to be prepared for 40 years in Egypt and 40 years in the wilderness before God used him to deliver Israel from Egyptian bondage. I don't know why Naomi faced such adversity for all those years until God provided an heir to be in the lineage of the Messiah. I don't know why Hannah was humiliated year after year until God blessed her with the birth of Samuel—one of the greatest Old Testament prophets. I don't know why David had to wait so many years to actually become king over all Israel after being anointed king by Samuel.

I don't know why Jeremiah was so mistreated in the midst of his being completely faithful and obedient to God. I don't know why Mary had to suffer deep anguish of soul watching Jesus' suffering and death, even though she was blessed to be His mother, and believed what God said would be accomplished. I don't know why it was prophesied that Jesus' body would stay in the tomb for three days, while the disciples lost all faith and hope. I don't know why Paul was left blind for three days after the Damascus road experience before receiving his sight.

I don't always know why God works in the time or way He does. But I do know that God is faithful, and in His time and way, He will accomplish His purpose.

We gain much insight from the account of Jesus' delay in visiting Lazarus, whose sickness resulted in death. Jesus loved Lazarus and his two sisters, Mary and Martha, yet when He heard Lazarus was sick, He remained where He was two additional days. This delay seemed like apparent indifference and unconcern for a family whom He loved and who dearly loved and honored Him. Lazarus' sisters suffered much sorrow and emotional anguish which Jesus could have alleviated if He hadn't purposely delayed His arrival and healed Lazarus before he died.

This temporary tragedy was allowed so that God would be glorified, Jesus' disciples' faith increased, and all believers in Christ would be provided a profound hope of resurrection and eternal life. Although Jesus' timing and purpose was different from what Mary and Martha wanted, it proved to bring a greater victory in the end than if Lazarus would have been healed as they desired. In the midst of our trials, God's timing and will may be different than what we anticipate or would like. However, His wisdom and love always prove best in the end.

I have told many believers who wanted to run away from a difficult situation that:

> God often does not change our circumstances until we learn to live victoriously in the midst of them.

The Lord wants people who will strive to honor Him—day after day after day—no matter what their circumstances.

An Unexpected Answer

I had just finished lifting weights and playing trampoline basketball with a bunch of guys at our ministry center when we decided to play football frenzy, a game I invented. An hour and a half earlier, I had just ended a day's fast during which I was seeking the Lord for healing and other things. (Since a car accident over two-and-a-half years earlier in Oregon, I had been going through therapy for my neck. It helped, but I still had very limited mobility.)

During the game of football frenzy, I was guarding my younger brother. He faked to the left, so I followed, and then he turned full speed in the opposite direction and hit me so hard on my left cheek with his forehead that my head snapped back. I heard about six or seven loud grinding cracks in my neck. My left eye went blurry and I heard a ringing in my left ear. My left cheek quickly began to swell.

After checking the mirror to see how bad the damage was, I finished playing the game. My left cheekbone remained sore for almost two weeks. After the soreness disappeared, I noticed that I regained much of the mobility I had lost since the car accident. I could bend my head back to shave without much discomfort. A few days after that football game, I got on the trampoline and did backflips for the first time in two-and-a-half years. I still have occasional neck pain to remind me I was in a bad car accident, but it is greatly improved.

God is amazing! There is no way a doctor could have hit me hard enough to crack my neck the way my brother did. He had to hit me at exactly the right speed and angle, and at the exact location on my cheek necessary to accomplish that. While the Lord didn't heal my neck when or how I expected, in His time and way, I am convinced that He lined up the circumstances to answer that prayer.

A Proper Attitude

When the 12 spies sent out to gather information about the Promised Land and its occupants returned to Moses, they reported that they saw giants in the land. Moses himself had told the spies to see what the land was like, whether the people who lived there were strong or weak, and if the towns they lived in were unwalled or fortified (Numbers 13:17-20).

So why does Scripture indicate that 10 of the spies gave what God called an evil report, while the report of Joshua and Caleb was called good? The 10 spies were afraid of the giants and didn't believe God's promise that He would give them the land (Numbers 13:2). They said—

> We can't attack those people; they are stronger than we are. The land we explored devours those living in it. All the people we saw there are of great size. We saw the Nephilim there (the descendants of Anak come from the Nephilim). We seemed like grasshoppers in our own eyes, and we looked the same to them (Numbers 13:31-33).

As a result of the faithless report that was spread among the Israelites by the fearful spies, the people grumbled in their tents—

> The Lord hates us; so He brought us out of Egypt to deliver us into the hands of the Amorites to destroy us. Where can we go? Our brothers have made us lose heart. They say, "The people are stronger and taller than we are; the cities are large, with walls up to the sky. We even saw the Anakites there" (Deuteronomy 1:27,28).

Their statement that the Lord hated them could not have been further from the truth. They would later learn that even while in the desert as consequence of their sin, the Lord was with them and carried them as a father carries a son (Deuteronomy 1:31). He watched over them in the vast desert and saw that they lacked nothing (Deuteronomy 2:7)—not even their clothes nor sandals wore out, nor did their feet swell (Deuteronomy 8:4; 29:5; Nehemiah 9:21).

Nevertheless, the devastating report of the 10 spies caused the Israelites to lose heart and the people began to murmur and complain.

> That night all the people of the community raised their voices and wept aloud. All the Israelites grumbled against Moses and Aaron, and the whole assembly said to them, "If only we had died in Egypt! Or in this desert! Why is the Lord bringing us to this land only to let us fall by the sword? Our wives and children will be taken as plunder. Wouldn't it be better for us to go back to Egypt?" And they said to each other, "We should choose a leader and go back to Egypt" (Numbers 14:1-4).

They were actually going to stone Moses, Aaron, Joshua, and Caleb, until the Lord intervened (Numbers 14:10).

The Israelites praised the Lord when they saw Him do such incredible things as:

- the miraculous signs and wonders in Egypt
- the parting of the Red Sea
- the pillar of cloud by day and the pillar of fire by night
- the water that came from the rock in the wilderness
- the manna from heaven they were given to eat.

But how soon they forgot God's mighty acts on their behalf and His faithfulness in the past. Refusing to trust His promises concerning their future, they began to grumble, complain, and rebel when circumstances were less than ideal or they faced difficulties and saw giants.

> The Lord said to Moses, "How long will these people treat Me with contempt? How long will they refuse to believe in Me, in spite of all the miraculous signs I have performed among them?" (Numbers 14:11).

Christians today also have that same natural inclination. Many believers only praise the Lord when He is blessing them. When they face obstacles or when God doesn't do what they want, they lose heart and become discouraged and defeated.

While on a spiritual high or a mountaintop experience, they love the Lord. But when they are inconvenienced or encounter *giants*, many murmur, complain, have a bad attitude, and turn away from the Lord in rebellion.

Numbers 14:20-38 gives God's insightful response following Moses' powerful intercession for Him not to destroy the Israelites—

> The Lord replied, "I have forgiven them, as you asked. Nevertheless, as surely as I live and

as surely as the glory of the Lord fills the whole earth, not one of the men who saw My glory and the miraculous signs I performed in Egypt and in the desert but who disobeyed Me and tested Me ten times—not one of them will ever see the land I promised on oath to their forefathers. No one who has treated Me with contempt will ever see it. But because My servant Caleb has a different spirit and follows Me wholeheartedly, I will bring him into the land he went to, and his descendants will inherit it. Since the Amalekites and Canaanites are living in the valleys, turn back tomorrow and set out toward the desert along the route to the Red Sea."

The Lord said to Moses and Aaron: "How long will this wicked community grumble against Me? I have heard the complaints of these grumbling Israelites. So tell them, 'As surely as I live, declares the Lord, I will do to you the very things I heard you say: In this desert your bodies will fall—every one of you twenty years old or more who was counted in the census and who has grumbled against Me. Not one of you will enter the land I swore with uplifted hand to make your home, except Caleb son of Jephunneh and Joshua son of Nun.

As for your children that you said would be taken as plunder, I will bring them in to enjoy the land you have rejected. But you—your bodies will fall in this desert. Your children will be shepherds here for forty years, suffering for your unfaithfulness, until the last of your bodies lies in the desert. For forty years—one year for each of the forty days you explored the land—you will suffer for your sins and know what it is like to have Me against you.' I, the Lord, have spoken, and I will surely do these things to this whole wicked community, which has banded together against Me. They will meet their end in this desert; here they will die."

So the men Moses had sent to explore the land, who returned and made the whole community grumble against Him by spreading a bad report about it—these men responsible for spreading the bad report about the land were struck down and died of a plague before the Lord. Of the men who went to explore the land, only Joshua son of Nun and Caleb son of Jephunneh survived.

God desires believers who not only praise Him when the excitement and the miracles are occurring, but also trust, praise, and honor Him when facing *giants* or adverse circumstances.

I was speaking at an Arabic church to people from several Moslem countries who knew first-hand suffering and persecution for Christ. One Iraqi man who had acted as a translator for Saddam Hussein during Desert Storm told me that when the U.S. was so accurately hitting Iraqi targets, he was falsely accused of providing secret information to the Allies. While he was being beaten, his attackers stopped when they noticed that he was smiling. He shared with them how he was blessed to suffer for Christ. (After the war, he and his pregnant wife fled Iraq to Jordan then came to America.)

We Can't Lose

My son, who was 20 at the time, had just finished practice for the high school soccer team he coached. For a few minutes we sat together on a swing overlooking the ministry center's property. The trees were a lush green, and birds were flying overhead against a backdrop of brilliant blue sky. As we pondered the beauty all around us, I remarked, "The heavens declare the glory of our God, and He created us to glorify Him. When we seek to honor Him with all our hearts and in everything we do, it will go well for us in the end." I have learned a crucial lesson: When I honor the Lord, I can't lose. When I dishonor Him, I can't win.

Entrusting Tabitha into the Lord's Care

On Mother's Day, May 11,1997 (10 years to the day my father died), my daughter Tabitha moved to San Diego, California (just about the farthest place in the U.S. from her home in Pennsylvania). It was most difficult to see her go, because along with our son, B.J., she has been the joy of our lives as well as a great asset to the ministry—the most wonderful daughter a parent could ask for. We were losing a daughter, best friend, and staff worker whose bubbling love, joy, and enthusiasm livened up the ministry center and encouraged all who met her. She also helped me with the 10 books I was writing simultaneously for the prior two years—one of the hardest tasks I have ever done.

We had almost lost Tabitha once before to Paraguay when she did her student teaching for college. She had contemplated staying permanently. But now our beautiful, vivacious daughter was definitely moving to San Diego. Our lives would never be the same. Tabitha and her mom sang a duet at church on Mother's Day, and then we went out to eat as a family in Akron, Ohio, from where we said our goodbyes.

Tabitha had been earnestly seeking the Lord's direction for her life for the past two years and felt He was leading her to San Diego. The Lord has been so faithful to us in the past, how could we now not trust Him with our future? Although she was facing many overwhelming obstacles, I knew that if the Lord was in it, no obstacle could thwart His plan.

God's Plan Unfolds

As the Psalmist says—

> Since You are my rock and my fortress, for the sake of Your name lead and guide me (Psalms 31:3).

And so it was with Tabitha. After seeking employment for over a month while staying at her cousin's apartment in San Diego, the Lord moved. Tabitha was hired at the very school she had desired and for the teaching position (second grade) she had hoped for, being chosen from many other applicants. This couldn't have come at a better time. According to apartment policy, she had stayed close to the end of her allotted time and would soon have to vacate the premises. Where would she live now that she had a teaching position and had to leave her cousin's apartment? She prayed about it. As she was waiting for God's answer to her prayers and contemplating her possibilities, an apartment opened up unexpectedly right below her cousin's apartment and next door to her future fiance, Clayton Smith, giving her the perfect living location.

Clayton ended up becoming the husband Tabitha had prayed for so earnestly and waited for so patiently. A little less than a year after being married, they bought a house in San Diego. They offered us a portion of it to be used for a West Coast branch of our ministry. As Joseph had gone to Egypt to prepare the way for his family, so the Lord had led Tabitha to San Diego to prepare the way.

Believe God and Live

We all face *giants*! The determining factor is not the *giants* we face. Most important is the attitude we have while facing those *giants*. If we think that the *giants* in our lives are impossible to overcome, we are already defeated. When we have faith in the Lord, we know that no matter what circumstances prevail, they will work out for good and we will ultimately be victorious.

My main goal during our ministry center building projects was for the Lord to be glorified and for people to see that the Lord brought it about—not us. I assumed that everything would go smoothly all the time. I didn't expect problems or financial shortages—

just miracle after miracle. The Lord spoke to my heart that even more than the miracles He performed, He is glorified when we, in the midst of difficult conditions and obstacles, still trust, praise, and honor Him.

It is easy to thank the Lord and testify when things are going well or after a goal is reached or a miraculous intervention occurs. But He wants us to have an attitude of trust and thanksgiving even when we face perplexing problems—before our goal and victory looks possible.

I had many speaking engagements during our building projects, and even though we were low on funds or in tough circumstances, I always acknowledged my trust in the Lord and assured the people that God would somehow enable us to finish the construction He had led us to do. And He was faithful to do so.

Murmuring Can Be Dangerous

Murmuring and complaining before the Lord is very dangerous. The 10 spies who gave a bad report (causing the people to grumble) were struck down and died of a plague (Numbers 14:36,37). It was because the people murmured and rebelled that they had to wander in the wilderness for 40 years (Numbers 14:20-35).

When we murmur and complain today, we are left to wander in frustration. Complaining also drains our health and vitality and renders us ineffective. It produces a negative testimony for the Lord.

God explicitly warns New Testament believers that His judgment on Israel for her unbelief and disobedience should serve as a warning to us (I Corinthians 10:1-11). Hebrews 3:7-19 contains a strong admonition for believers today—

> So, as the Holy Spirit says: "Today, if you hear His voice, do not harden your hearts as you did in the rebellion, during the time of testing in

the desert, where your fathers tested and tried Me and for forty years saw what I did. That is why I was angry with that generation, and I said, 'Their hearts are always going astray, and they have not known My ways.' So I declared on oath in My anger, 'They shall never enter My rest.'"

See to it, brothers, that none of you has a sinful, unbelieving heart that turns away from the living God. But encourage one another daily, as long as it is called Today, so that none of you may be hardened by sin's deceitfulness. We have come to share in Christ if we hold firmly till the end the confidence we had at first. As has just been said: "Today, if you hear His voice, do not harden your hearts as you did in the rebellion."

Who were they who heard and rebelled? Were they not all those Moses led out of Egypt? And with whom was He angry for forty years? Was it not with those who sinned, whose bodies fell in the desert? And to whom did God swear that they would never enter His rest if not to those who disobeyed? So we see that they were not able to enter, because of their unbelief.

Hebrews 4:11—

Let us, therefore, make every effort to enter that rest, so that no one will fall by following their example of disobedience.

It wasn't until that generation of murmurers were dead in the wilderness that Joshua and Caleb and the new generation of Israelites were brought into the Promised Land.

Are You Willing to Be Humiliated, for the Lord to Be Glorified?

As I endured one obstacle after another and as I suffered one apparent defeat after the other with no hope of victory in sight, I asked, "Why Lord, are you allowing me to be humiliated? This is completely opposite to what You had promised." He spoke to my heart: "Are you willing to be humiliated that I may be glorified?" Then he spoke to my heart to review the heroes of the faith recorded in Scripture—they all suffered apparent humiliation before He greatly used them and fulfilled His promise to them. I said, "Yes, Lord I am willing to be humiliated for You to be glorified." After months of apparent defeat and humiliation, He intervened and fulfilled His promise and brought about a great victory.

I later realized that I had more impact on people's lives through these seemingly humiliating times than if it would have been merely easy victories. Many commented concerning my attitude of faith and trust and peace in the midst of the storm that the light of the Lord shone all the brighter in contrast to the apparent darkness of my circumstances.

Trusting God Leads to Victory

Joshua and Caleb had acknowledged that there were giants in the land, but God called their report good. Why? They knew that the giants were real, and that they were strong and intimidating. But instead of comparing the giants to themselves, they compared them to the awesome and all-powerful God they served. Caleb said—

> We should go up and take possession of the land, for we can certainly do it (Numbers 13:30).

Then both Joshua and Caleb said—

> Do not rebel against the Lord. And do not be afraid of the people of the land, because we will swallow them up. Their protection is gone, but the Lord is with us. Do not be afraid of them (Numbers 14:9).

Joshua and Caleb knew it looked impossible, but they also knew that their God could do the impossible and that He would be faithful to fulfill what He had promised.

Our proper Biblical attitude should be:

> I know my *giants* are real. But the God I serve is greater than any *giant*, problem, obstacle, or opposition I encounter. Through Him I can and eventually will overcome every *giant* I face.

It is usually not our *giants* that defeat us, but our *fear* of the *giants.* Either your fear will erode your faith in the Lord, or your faith will overcome your fear. You must decide whether you will be victimized by fear and unbelief or whether you will overcome your fear and doubt through faith and trust in the Lord.

We learn from the illustration about King Saul that God expects us to trust Him and obey Him no matter what our circumstances. I Samuel 13:5-14 indicates that the Philistines, with an army as numerous as the sand on the seashore, were assembled to fight Israel. Samuel had not arrived at the appointed time to offer sacrifice for the Lord's favor, and Saul's army was scattering from him. The situation was so desperate that Saul felt compelled to offer the sacrifice himself. Samuel arrived just as Saul finished making the offering, and severely rebuked Saul for disobeying the Lord's command. Saul also disobeyed other commands of God, and as a result, God rejected Saul as king.

No matter what our circumstances, we must trust and obey.

A storm on the Sea of Galilee almost caused the disciples' boat to perish in the waves. They were terrified. Jesus rebuked them for having so little faith. Luke 8:23-25 gives the following account—

As they sailed, He fell asleep. A squall came down on the lake, so that the boat was being swamped, and they were in great danger. The disciples went and woke Him, saying, "Master, Master, we're going to drown!" He got up and rebuked the wind and the raging waters; the storm subsided, and all was calm. "Where is your faith?" He asked His disciples....

In the midst of a situation in which they were about to perish, Jesus still expected them to trust Him. Trusting God requires faith.

Hebrews 11:1,2—

Now faith is being sure of what we hope for and certain of what we do not see. This is what the ancients were commended for.

Hebrews 11:6—

And without faith it is impossible to please God, because anyone who comes to Him must believe that He exists and that He rewards those who earnestly seek Him.

Hebrews 11:32-39—

And what more shall I say? I do not have time to tell about Gideon, Barak, Samson, Jephthah, David, Samuel and the prophets, who through faith conquered kingdoms, administered justice, and gained what was promised; who shut the mouths of lions, quenched the fury of the flames, and escaped the edge of the sword; whose weakness was turned to strength; and who became powerful in battle and routed foreign armies.

Women received back their dead, raised to life again. Others were tortured and refused to be released, so that they might gain a better resurrection. Some faced jeers and flogging, while still others were chained and put in prison.

They were stoned; they were sawed in two; they were put to death by the sword. They went about in sheepskins and goatskins, destitute, persecuted and mistreated—the world was not worthy of them. They wandered in deserts and mountains, and in caves and holes in the ground.

These were all commended for their faith....

Always Trust Him—No Matter What

The Lord teaches us through our circumstances to always trust Him no matter what. For example, during the early days of my ministry, I was to speak at a church over an hour away. We were supposed to be there by 9:30 a.m. and absolutely no later than 10:30 a.m. Karen and I took our children to stay with my sister the night before. My younger brother and another teen who helped with our media equipment stayed all night so we could get an early start.

We had our van loaded and our team was ready to go at 8:00 a.m., so we could arrive in plenty of time to set up. But the van wouldn't start. After a few minutes and several tries, it started momentarily, but then it stalled and wouldn't start again. A neighbor just happened to walk out of his door. He tried to jump-start the van, but while doing so, the pressure plate went out and the clutch pedal stuck to the floor, making it impossible to drive. Calling to cancel wasn't even an option. I had never before missed a speaking engagement, and I was determined not to then.

We thought we could borrow a station wagon or van, but when we called to do so we were informed that one friend's van had a blown engine and another friend couldn't start her station wagon because it was so cold. Finally, we located an available station wagon. A neighbor gave me a ride to get it, but when we got there it wouldn't start either. After trying to locate jumper cables for 10 minutes, I told the owner to forget it, since I noticed the car also had a flat tire. So our ride took us back to our apartment.

Ironically, I was supposed to speak that day on Romans 8:28, *Life in the Pressure Cooker*—how all things "work together for good to those who love God, to those who are called according to His purpose"(NAS). The Lord seemed to be asking, "Do you really believe what you are going to preach?" I said, "Yes!"

At 9:15 a.m. we still had no transportation, but the Lord spoke to my heart, "Trust Me." So we held hands, prayed, and decided that no matter what, we would have a good attitude and not murmur and complain. The Lord then brought to my mind a person to call. So Karen telephoned this person whose sister just happened to have a station wagon we could borrow. They brought it to our apartment and we had it loaded by 9:35 a.m. We arrived at the church at 10:35 a.m. We had just enough time to get everything ready. In spite of the seemingly impossible circumstances and a frustrating morning, the service went great, and as a result of the morning message and the evening media presentation, the church put our ministry on their missions budget.

One of the reminders on my prayer and fasting list is to ask the Lord to:

> Forgive me and help me overcome impatience, a bad attitude, murmuring, complaining, and rebelling, by replacing them with patience, endurance, perseverance, determination, faithfulness, and an attitude of trusting, praising, and honoring Him no matter what.

For every obstacle I face, for every promise I am trusting Him to fulfill, and for every time I believe that He is leading me to do something, I want my prayer to be, "Lord, help me to have:

- Unwavering faith to believe and trust You
- Sensitivity, discernment, and wisdom concerning what to do and how to do it
- Obedience, so I will do it

- Motivation and determination, so I will persevere
- The attitude You want me to have
- An understanding of the lessons You want me to learn
- The opportunity and circumstances to bring it about in Your time and way
- Your courage, strength, power, anointing, and authority to do it
- And may the end result be blessing and ultimate victory for Your honor and glory."

God's Boot Camp

The Lord had a monumental task for Moses—leading an ungrateful, unbelieving, murmuring, complaining, rebellious people from Egyptian bondage through many hardships to the Promised Land. On occasion, Moses cried out to the Lord that the task was too hard (Numbers 11:10-15). Even the Lord became angry with these grumbling people on several occasions (Numbers 11:1,10; 12:9; 14:11...). But God had taken Moses through a personalized boot camp—40 years in Egypt and 40 years in the wilderness—and Moses was prepared to fulfill God's purpose.

Moses spent the last 40 years of his life leading the Israelites in the desert until all the men who were of military age when they left Egypt had died (Joshua 5:6). Those years in the desert also served as a boot camp for the next generation of Israelites who would inherit the Promised Land—

> Remember how the Lord your God led you all the way in the desert these forty years, to humble you and to test you in order to know what was in your heart, whether or not you would

keep His commands. He humbled you, causing you to hunger and then feeding you with manna, which neither you nor your fathers had known, to teach you that man does not live on bread alone but on every word that comes from the mouth of the Lord.

He led you through the vast and dreadful desert, that thirsty and waterless land, with its venomous snakes and scorpions. He brought you water out of hard rock. He gave you manna to eat in the desert, something your fathers had never known, to humble and to test you so that in the end it might go well with you (Deuteronomy 8:2,3,15,16).

God's Boot Camp Is Not Pleasant

I used to run total fitness classes and defense clinics. I developed various drills and rigorous training methods to teach the students discipline and determination. One of the drills I did was to line everyone up and spar them one after another for one to three minutes. Sometimes I would spar with two or three of them at the same time. Then I had them do the same thing among themselves. I did this to make them strong and to develop their endurance, so they would be able to deal with almost any attack situation. So too, God desires to mold us so that we can stand in any situation and face and overcome any obstacle.

One teenager, who had moved to Colorado with his family, came back for a month to Pennsylvania in the summer. He said to me, "Bill, I am going into the Army. You have one month to do whatever you want to get me in shape." I said, "I will do it if you agree to totally obey me and do everything I ask without complaining." He agreed.

I made him jog several miles a day, bike, jump on a trampoline, do pushups, pullups, and situps, lift weights, box and spar me and other people, run obstacle courses, and do other rigorous training. He wrote a letter thanking me because he was able to handle basic training with much greater ease than most of the other soldiers.

God has a boot camp that is far more rigorous than the military, the martial arts, or Olympic training. He trains us in the *wilderness* and *desert*.

Joseph, Moses, Naomi, Ruth, David, Daniel, Paul—all the heroes of the faith—went through their personalized boot camp as they faced numerous obstacles and difficulties. At the time, I am certain they would have loved to avoid them, but they later proved to be the very means by which the Lord prepared them for the purpose He had.

At times, I have wondered why God makes it so hard for so long. But I realize that when I was a coach in soccer, I trained my players harder than anyone else. As a result, we won four championships during the four years I coached youth soccer. When I was a fitness instructor at a health spa, they called me a drill sergeant because I worked them so hard. When I taught self-defense and karate (before the Lord led me out of it), I made it harder than any instructor had made it on me, because I wanted them to be able to handle any situation on the street.

In your walk with the Lord, remember:

- If you want the *mountaintops,* you must go through the *valleys.*
- If you want the *green pasture and still waters*, you must endure the *wilderness.*
- If you want the *oasis*, you must cross the *desert.*
- If you want *spiritual power*, you must develop *spiritual muscles.*
- If you want *victories*, you must *fight battles.*
- If you want *to see God do the impossible,*

then you must *stand in faith in impossible situations.*

Valleys and Mountaintops

The *miracles* let us know that a real and personal God is working in our lives and ministries. These are our mountaintop experiences. They are exciting and rejuvenating. They encourage us and build faith, as well as give our faith validity in the eyes of an unbelieving skeptical world. In this way, others see that our God is real and that He intervenes in the lives of those who are obedient to His will.

When we face *giants,* obstacles, and difficulties; when we feel trapped in dark *valleys,* barren *wildernesses,* or parched *deserts,* that is when our character is molded, our faith and determination are built, and our strength and spiritual muscles developed. It is then that our testimony shines forth most brightly to the world. They see our faith which stands the test. They realize that, like Job, "Though He slay me, yet will I hope in Him" (Job 13:15).

Stranded in the Judean Wilderness

During a Middle East outreach to Jordan, Israel, and Egypt, I had a free day between my evening speaking engagements in Jerusalem.

I caught a bus in Jerusalem to head to Ein Gedi on the west side of the Dead Sea. On the bus were many Israeli soldiers and civilians. I got off the bus at the wrong spot. Stranded near a small resort on the Dead Sea, I tried to catch a ride south to my destination, but no one was heading that direction. One of the workers who was leaving realized my dilemma and offered me a ride part of the way. She said, "I am probably not doing you a favor, but if you wait at the bus stop (four posts, a small roof, and a bench) where I leave you and point your hand to the road, someone will pick you up."

I was stranded in the Judean desert by the Dead Sea for an hour and a half. It was hot, dry, barren, desolate, rugged terrain. Except for an occasional vehicle which whizzed by in spite of my trying to hitch a ride, it was a lonely place.

At first I questioned, "What am I doing here, Lord? Why did You let me end up here?" Then He spoke to my heart to look around. I realized that many a man of God was molded in this rugged, remote desert and wilderness—and places like it.

I spent some time praying and reflecting on the terrain and circumstances God used to shape many of the heroes of the faith—not for merely an hour and a half, but often for months and even years.

After an hour and a half, when it appeared no one would give me a ride, a bus stopped at the remote bus stop. I jumped on and discovered I was only a few miles from my intended destination, which proved to be an oasis in the rugged desert.

Giants Help Develop Spiritual Muscles

Giants and obstacles are like exercise. Exercise works because of resistance. The greater the resistance, the bigger and stronger your muscles become. The more *giants* we face, the more character and spiritual muscles we develop.

Usually, what I have wanted God to deliver me from is what has eventually made me the strongest. Something happens in the *wilderness*, *valley*, and *desert* that does not happen on the *mountaintop*; God builds character, strength, faith, and determination, and molds lives to accomplish His purpose.

On the way home from seeing a specialist after my son injured his knee for the second time while playing soccer, and there was no alternative but to face extensive surgery, I told him that, "Trials, obstacles, and difficulties put iron in our blood and make us strong as nails."

For about 10 years during our early Christian lives and ministry, Karen and I lived in extreme poverty. It looked as though we would never have anything. Over the years we faced many hard times, difficulties, obstacles, *giants*, and impossible circumstances, but the Lord somehow always intervened in His time and way to enable us to overcome them.

I often wondered why all my Christian life and in our ministry, God permitted so many difficult times. We seemed to have to do everything the hard way. Yet, God has taught me the reality of all things working together for good to those who love Him and are called according to His purpose (Romans 8:28). I have walked with the Lord more than 28 years, and I can honestly testify to the truth and reality of this Scriptural promise.

I am glad to have persevered for so long through our impoverished beginnings and many hard times. Since the Lord has greatly blessed my life and ministry, no one can say that I only serve Him for all the blessings He has given me. I served the Lord when we had nothing, and no hope of ever having anything, and I serve the Lord when He blesses me. I will also serve Him if He takes away everything He has given to me, like He did to Job. I have served Him—and will continue to—no matter what.

Don't Let Prosperity Affect Your Memory

We must not forget that many fall away from the Lord during times of prosperity. Therefore, let us heed Moses' warning to those Israelites who were about to enter the Promised Land—

> When you have eaten and are satisfied, praise the Lord your God for the good land He has given you. Be careful that you do not forget the Lord your God, failing to observe His commands, His laws and His decrees that I am giving you this day. Otherwise, when you eat and are satisfied, when you build fine houses and

settle down, and when your herds and flocks grow large and your silver and gold increase and all you have is multiplied, then your heart will become proud and you will forget the Lord your God, who brought you out of Egypt, out of the land of slavery (Deuteronomy 8:10-14).

Hosea 13:4-9 reveals the consequences of forgetting the Lord in times of being satisfied —

But I am the Lord your God, who brought you out of Egypt. You shall acknowledge no God but Me, no Savior except Me. I cared for you in the desert, in the land of burning heat. When I fed them, they were satisfied; when they were satisfied, they became proud; then they forgot Me. So I will come upon them like a lion, like a leopard I will lurk by the path. Like a bear robbed of her cubs, I will attack them and rip them open. Like a lion I will devour them; a wild animal will tear them apart. You are destroyed, O Israel, because you are against Me, against your Helper.

Deuteronomy 8:5 encourages us—

Know then in your heart that as a man disciplines his son, so the Lord your God disciplines you.

Hebrews 12:5-11—

And you have forgotten that word of encouragement that addresses you as sons:

"My son, do not make light of the Lord's discipline, and do not lose heart when He rebukes you, because the Lord disciplines those He loves, and He punishes everyone He accepts as a son."

Endure hardship as discipline; God is treating you as sons. For what son is not disciplined by his father? If you are not disciplined (and everyone undergoes discipline), then you are illegitimate children and not true sons. Moreover, we have all had human fathers who disciplined us and we respected them for it. How much more should we submit to the Father of our spirits and live!

Our fathers disciplined us for a little while as they thought best; but God disciplines us for our good, that we may share in His holiness. No discipline seems pleasant at the time, but painful. Later on, however, it produces a harvest of righteousness and peace for those who have been trained by it.

Revelation 3:19—

Those whom I love I rebuke and discipline. So be earnest, and repent.

Psalm 103:8-13—

The Lord is compassionate and gracious, slow to anger, abounding in love. He will not always accuse, nor will He harbor His anger forever; He does not treat us as our sins deserve or repay us according to our iniquities. For as high as the heavens are above the earth, so great is His love for those who fear Him; as far as the east is from the west, so far has He removed our transgressions from us. As a father has compassion on his children, so the Lord has compassion on those who fear Him.

The Lord often hides His face and allows us to go through hard times so that we will seek Him with all our hearts and always be dependent upon Him. He makes us strong so we will not buckle when under pressure, but will endure and honor Him through any circumstance. He prepares those He loves through His various *boot camps* that we might fulfill the purpose He has for our lives.

Achieving
Ultimate Victory

While ministering in Florida one February, we were staying in the Fort Myers area with friends. Before leaving, the husband asked me to go into the swamp with him. He said, "It will be a challenge—and we will see some alligators and snakes." I asked the Lord and my wife, and then said, "Okay, I'll go with you." When I responded affirmatively, he said, "You know Bill, I used to think you were crazy, but now I know you are crazy. Nobody who has visited me before has been willing to go into the swamp."

We went into the swamp and waded through cold water. It gradually became deeper, until it was above our waists. We had to feel our way along the bottom of the murky swamp water with our feet to avoid tripping over tree roots and stumps—and to avoid falling into any holes. In the process, I banged up my shin and fell into a few holes.

We enjoyed getting to see exotic birds (and hawks and owls), but we also had to cautiously watch the trees above our heads for poisonous snakes and spider webs. We had to scan the top of the water for alligators and watch the brush areas lest we should get too close to their nests, causing the mother alligators to become aggressive.

We were in waist-to-chest-deep water and often-times, we were out in the open with no trees to climb. We were vulnerable to any alligator that might decide to attack us, because we were in too deep to kick and protect ourselves. We walked around under these conditions for an hour. (I later learned that February is not the time of year female alligators have babies, but that didn't lessen the stress factor at the time.)

I compare going through that swamp with walking with the Lord. You and I are going to face many dangers, difficulties, obstacles, challenges, and adventures.

Before I was a Christian, I tried almost every thrill imaginable. But I discovered that living for the Lord is the most exciting, challenging, and adventurous lifestyle available. If you don't believe me, ask those who have gone on mission trips with me!

God never promised He would remove all of our *giants*, and He didn't promise us an easy lifestyle. He did promise, however, to always be with us.

God Is Always There

In the autumn of the year, my wife Karen and I traveled to Colorado Springs on a ministry trip accompanied by a couple who serve on our staff. Because of dense fog, we arrived several hours late. We were forced to land in Denver first because the plane was running out of fuel from circling Colorado Springs waiting for the fog to lift. The dense fog, which shut down the airport, finally lifted and we were able to fly into Colorado Springs from Denver.

For our sleeping accommodations, we had booked Town and Country Cottages located at the edge of the Rockies. They were reasonably priced and had a scenic view. (Key to this story is the fact that the AAA travel book on Colorado showed Town and Country as 5.2 miles from the highway, but as we later discovered the hard way, these cottages were only 0.3 miles away.)

We all were exhausted from the stressful flight, but were looking forward to a short drive (so we thought) into the foothills of the mountains. Karen loves the mountains—provided the roads are not too narrow, steep, or dangerous.

It was my turn to drive. Darkness and fog created poor visibility, making travel conditions dangerous as we headed toward the cottage where we would obtain some much-needed sleep.

Being in the mountains, we assumed there would be winding roads, but didn't anticipate such sharp and continuous bends. After only a mile and a half we came to a private gate. We backtracked a mile but were convinced that we had not gotten off the main road, so we turned around again. A car in front of us went through the private gate, so we pulled up to it. It opened, so I drove through, thinking it was a public access through a private area on the way to our cottage.

As we continued, the road got steeper with more bends and dangerous winding curves. The cliffs, as far as I could tell, appeared to be very high and extremely steep. The dirt road was muddy as we edged up the mountain hoping to see the sign for our cottage.

Karen was scared on the way up the mountain. She began to cry as we traveled higher and higher. I tried comforting her by assuring her that we would make it safely. The other couple also tried to encourage her.

We traveled the 5.2 miles based on the AAA book information, but no cottage was in sight. To get help with directions, I stopped a car that was coming in the opposite direction. We were told the cottage was way back down the mountain. They curiously asked how we had gotten through the gate onto private property.

Seeing no place to turn around, I used a section of the road to repeatedly, but cautiously, back up and pull forward so as not to go over the edge of the mountain. The trip down the mountainous road was even more treacherous. Wide awake from all the adrenaline, I clutched the steering wheel with my right hand, because my left hand and head were hanging out the window so I could see better. Karen was watching the road with great intensity and concern. Even the couple in the back seat had to help with guidance, alternately sticking their heads out the windows against the cold and rain.

The fog had become much denser. The muddy road, the side of the mountain, and the edge of the road often merged into one as I had a brief lapse of visibility around each descending curve. Although my speed was only five to ten miles an hour, as I came around every bend it was impossible to distinguish whether we were on the road, near the edge, about to run into the side of the mountain, or slide over the edge of the mountain. There was only a small mound of dirt about a foot high (which served as the only guardrail most of the way) which I used as a guide to keep us on the road.

(The lady who manned the gate told me the next day that Ripley of *Ripley's Believe It or Not* once said that the first mile after the gate is the most winding mile in America. We were also told that there are many dangerous drop-offs which are extremely steep and easy to go over in the dark.)

Although Karen did not want to return down the mountain, we had no choice. I kept repeating to her, "We're going to make it; I've got it under control. The Lord will protect us; we're going to be safe." And the Lord did get us down safely.

Isn't that the way it is with the Lord? Weary believers walking paths of danger and difficulty and wanting to give up are told by the Lord over and over to endure, persevere, and remain faithful. He is there with us and assures us that we will make it, that He will bring us safely through to our eternal Promised Land.

God did not deliver the Hebrew children from the fiery furnace, but He was with them in the midst of it. God did not save Daniel from being put into the lions' den, but He protected him while there. God did not smite Goliath before David encountered him, but He gave David the needed courage and strength to defeat him. God did not spare Joseph from being thrown into the pit, sold as a slave into Egypt, and locked up in a prison, but He was with him through it all. God did not save Stephen from being stoned, but He gave him the grace to endure it (Acts 7). God did not prevent Paul from being beaten, stoned, shipwrecked, and imprisoned, but He empowered him and furthered the Gospel through it.

God will also be with us. Psalm 46:1-3,7 promises—

> God is our refuge and strength, an ever-present help in trouble. Therefore we will not fear, though the earth give way and the mountains fall into the heart of the sea, though its waters roar and foam and the mountains quake with their surging. The Lord Almighty is with us; the God of Jacob is our fortress.

"Gliding" Through Life

During a Canadian and New England speaking tour, I stopped in New Hampshire. While there, I saw an article in a magazine entitled, *White Mountain Soaring*. It told about the exciting experience of going up in a glider plane (a plane without an engine).

I said, "Karen, it's my birthday. How about giving me a glider plane ride for a gift?" (We realized a few hours later that it wasn't really my birthday, it was only the 27th of July, not the 28th. You lose track of time when traveling.) So Karen gave me a gift of going up in a glider plane for fifteen minutes at Franconia Airport.

I sat in the very front of the glider plane and the pilot sat behind me. The pilot told me he wanted me to have a better view, but I doubted it. I knew that if we crashed I was a goner, because I was so close to the front. He told me that there was a lot of wind turbulence and that it would be bumpy, but that he would still take me up. They strapped me in extra tight.

Our glider plane was towed by another plane (with an engine) to about 3,000 feet. Then I heard a loud bang. I thought the front end of our plane had fallen off, but it was just the towline being released from our glider. There we were, two men 3,000 feet high with nothing but open air and the winds to keep us aloft. We were soaring through the air in a glider plane.

Sometimes it was as gentle as a ferris wheel, the wind gently lifting the whole plane up or moving it sideways. But other times it was as wild as a roller coaster. We would be hit by a gust of wind or the pilot would do a nose dive (pushing the nose of the glider toward the ground to build up air speed) and then pulling the nose up rather sharply. This "aerial roller coaster" provided a most exhilarating experience.

While we were less than 1,000 feet off the ground, going up and coming down was extremely bumpy because there was much wind turbulence. Above 1,000 feet was smooth (except for the few times the wind pushed the whole plane sideways or lifted it up or pushed it down).

To the west we could see into Vermont and to the east we could see into Maine. I once had a great fear of heights. But I believe in facing my fears and trusting the Lord to help me overcome them.

During the glider ride, I was enjoying myself, but I was also thinking:

> We're just floating aimlessly. There's no real purpose or direction to it. We're just going wherever the wind happens to take us. How is it all going to work out?

Many times in our walk with the Lord we feel like we are in a glider plane. We can see no purpose to it. We reason:

> I'm just floating aimlessly. I'm not growing. I'm not getting answers to prayer. It's never going to work out.

As we began our descent in that small glider plane, the turbulence increased in intensity. But guess what? Eventually the pilot guided that glider plane right down the center of the runway. He made a perfect landing. It turned out that we hadn't been floating aimlessly after all. There had been a purpose behind the whole thing, and it had worked out great.

If you are walking in obedience to His Word and yielded to His Spirit, there is a purpose for everything you go through. The Lord promises us that He will be faithful, and that everything will eventually work out for good. The end result will be ultimate victory!

Possessing the Land

The time finally came for the children of Israel to possess the land of Canaan which God had promised them as the descendants of Abraham, Isaac, and Jacob. Their desert wandering had finally come to an end. All those fighting men 20 years and older who had murmured were dead. Moses had also died, so his successor Joshua boldly led the new generation of Israelites into the land God had promised them.

Taking the land was no easy matter. Although the Lord helped Joshua and the Israelites achieve some amazing victories, they endured six years of fierce fighting before the 12 tribes found it safe to establish their dwellings in the land. As Moses said—

> The Lord your God will drive out those nations before you, little by little. You will not be allowed to eliminate them all at once, or the wild animals will multiply around you (Deuteronomy 7:22).

God fulfilled His word and gave the Promised Land to Abraham's descendants—

> So Joshua took the entire land, just as the Lord had directed Moses, and he gave it as an inheritance to Israel according to their tribal divisions (Joshua 11:23).

During the dividing of the land, Caleb, who was then 85 years old, reminded Joshua of the promise Moses had given him 45 years before—

> You know what the Lord said to Moses the man of God at Kadesh Barnea about you and me. I was forty years old when Moses the servant of the Lord sent me from Kadesh Barnea to explore the land. And I brought him back a report according to my convictions, but my brothers who went up with me made the hearts of the people melt with fear. I, however, followed the Lord my God wholeheartedly. So on that day Moses swore to me, "The land on which your feet have walked will be your inheritance and that of your children forever, because you have followed the Lord my God wholeheartedly."

> Now then, just as the Lord promised, He has kept me alive for forty-five years since the time He said this to Moses, while Israel moved about in the desert. So here I am today, eighty-five years old! I am still as strong today as the day Moses sent me out; I'm just as vigorous to go out

to battle now as I was then. Now give me this hill country that the Lord promised me that day. You yourself heard then that the Anakites were there and their cities were large and fortified, but, the Lord helping me, I will drive them out just as He said (Joshua 14:6-12).

Caleb knew that the report of the 10 spies, who kindled the flame of disbelief and rebellion, related primarily to the people and condition of this mountain area (Numbers 13:22,28,33). Forty-five years earlier Caleb earnestly attempted to convince the Israelites that they could defeat these powerful people, whose sight so distressed the 10 spies, and possess the land (Numbers 13:30). Now Caleb, knowing he must fight to drive out the Anakim, was as willing and able to do it as he was 45 years earlier. Though his enemies were well entrenched and had made the hill country a stronghold of giants, Caleb said to Joshua, "Give me this hill country." He knew his God was able to deliver it to him.

Joshua 14:13,14 states—

Then Joshua blessed Caleb son of Jephunneh and gave him Hebron as his inheritance. So Hebron has belonged to Caleb son of Jephunneh the Kenizzite ever since, because he followed the Lord, the God of Israel, wholeheartedly.

Joshua summoned all Israel and gave an exciting summation and warning—

The Lord has driven out before you great and powerful nations; to this day no one has been able to withstand you. One of you routs a thousand, because the Lord your God fights for you, just as He promised. So be very careful to love the Lord your God.

But if you turn away and ally yourselves with the survivors of these nations that remain among you and if you intermarry with them and associate with them, then you may be sure that the Lord your God will no longer drive out these nations before you. Instead, they will become snares and traps for you, whips on your backs and thorns in your eyes, until you perish from this good land, which the Lord your God has given you.

Now I am about to go the way of all the earth. You know with all your heart and soul that not one of all the good promises the Lord your God gave you has failed. Every promise has been fulfilled; not one has failed. But just as every good promise of the Lord your God has come true, so the Lord will bring on you all the evil He has threatened, until He has destroyed you from this good land He has given you. If you violate the covenant of the Lord your God, which He commanded you, and go and serve other gods and bow down to them, the Lord's anger will burn against you, and you will quickly perish from the good land He has given you (Joshua 23:9-16).

Take the Challenge

You have a choice today. You can be like the 10 spies, backing down in fear and defeat, murmuring, complaining, rebelling, and causing those around you to do the same. Or you can be like Joshua and Caleb—trusting, obeying, and honoring the Lord no matter what.

With the Lord's help, strength, and empowering, strive to:

- seek His will and not your own
- keep your eyes on Him, not on your circumstances
- be patient and faithful as God works in His time and way

- refuse to tolerate an attitude of murmuring and complaining
- obey and honor Him no matter what your circumstances
- submit as God takes you through His boot camp and develops your character and spiritual muscles
- trust Him with unwavering faith
- persevere until you overcome every *giant* and achieve ultimate victory.

FOR MORE INFORMATION:

Bill Rudge has produced numerous books, pamphlets, and cassettes on a variety of other timely topics. For a complete listing and a copy of his informative newsletter, write to:

Bill Rudge Ministries
P.O. Box 108
Sharon, PA 16146-0108
USA

www.billrudge.org